Mystic Mandalas

Geometrix 2

I0473115

Classic Patterns for Your
Adult Coloring Pleasure

by Randy Horn

www. SpectraGraf .com

ISBN-13:
978-0692684108 (SpectraGraf Publishing Co.)

ISBN-10:
0692684107

Introduction

Hi there!

I'm Randy and you are holding one of many in my line of Adult Coloring Books brought to you by www.SpectraGraf.com where you can find more great books and supplies for buckets of fun and relaxation, coloring to your heart's content.

(more on this in the back of this book)

Remember when you were just a kid and life was simple? Adult coloring books allow you to recapture those times when you can calm down, shift gears *and* create beautiful art often suitable for framing. So therapeutic.

The mandalas in this series were created with the colorist in mind. The first three volumes are as follows:

Geometrix – Graceful lines and arcs in geometric patterns.

Organix – Everyday objects rendered with an artistic flair.

Whymzykal – Fantastical images which sprang from our heads and landed splat on these pages!

More to come. Have a blast with them all… - Randy

Some tips on coloring your artwork:

1. Try using mixed-media for an even more diverse look, such as colored pencil in some areas mixed with watercolor washes in others.

2. When using crayons, try burnishing the wax with an artist's stump. In larger areas, burnish hard on the edges and lighten up toward the middle to create an almost stained glass look.

3. Always use the best materials you can afford. This doesn't necessarily mean "expensive". You'll find quality supplies at very reasonable prices at SpectraGraf. If you're going to spend hours creating your art, especially if you intend to frame some or all of them, don't waste your time with cheap colors.

4. Spend a couple bux on a color wheel. It will show you which colors are complimentary while giving you a better choice of color ranges… and they're cheap!

5. Try a monochromatic painting on one or more designs. This is where you choose various shades and tints of the same color, such as all blues. Strive for at least 3 shades/tints – light, medium and dark. The more you use, the nicer your artwork will be. Remember, white is a color, too.

6. Embellish some areas of the same shape and color with a little matching glitter for a more whimsical look!

7. When using watercolor, pre-wet the larger areas and drop pigment into the center or only paint the edges and let the pigment spread on its own. This is a *great* way to get a stained-glass look and feel to your paintings. You'll want to frame these, for sure.

8. Stop by the **SpectraShop** to pick up all your books and art supplies for endless coloring joy. Go here:

   http://spectragraf.com/spectrashop

*N*otes:

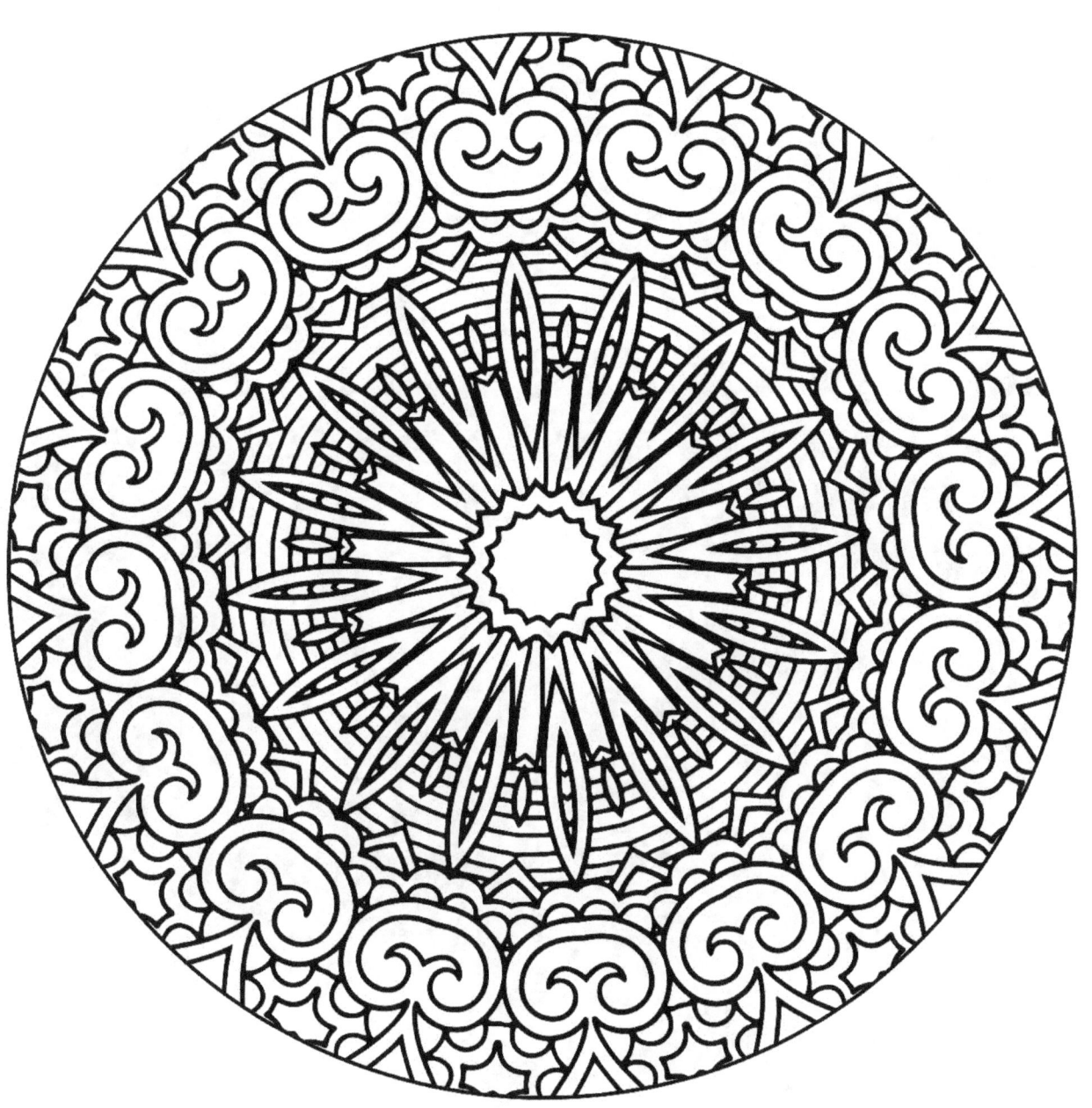

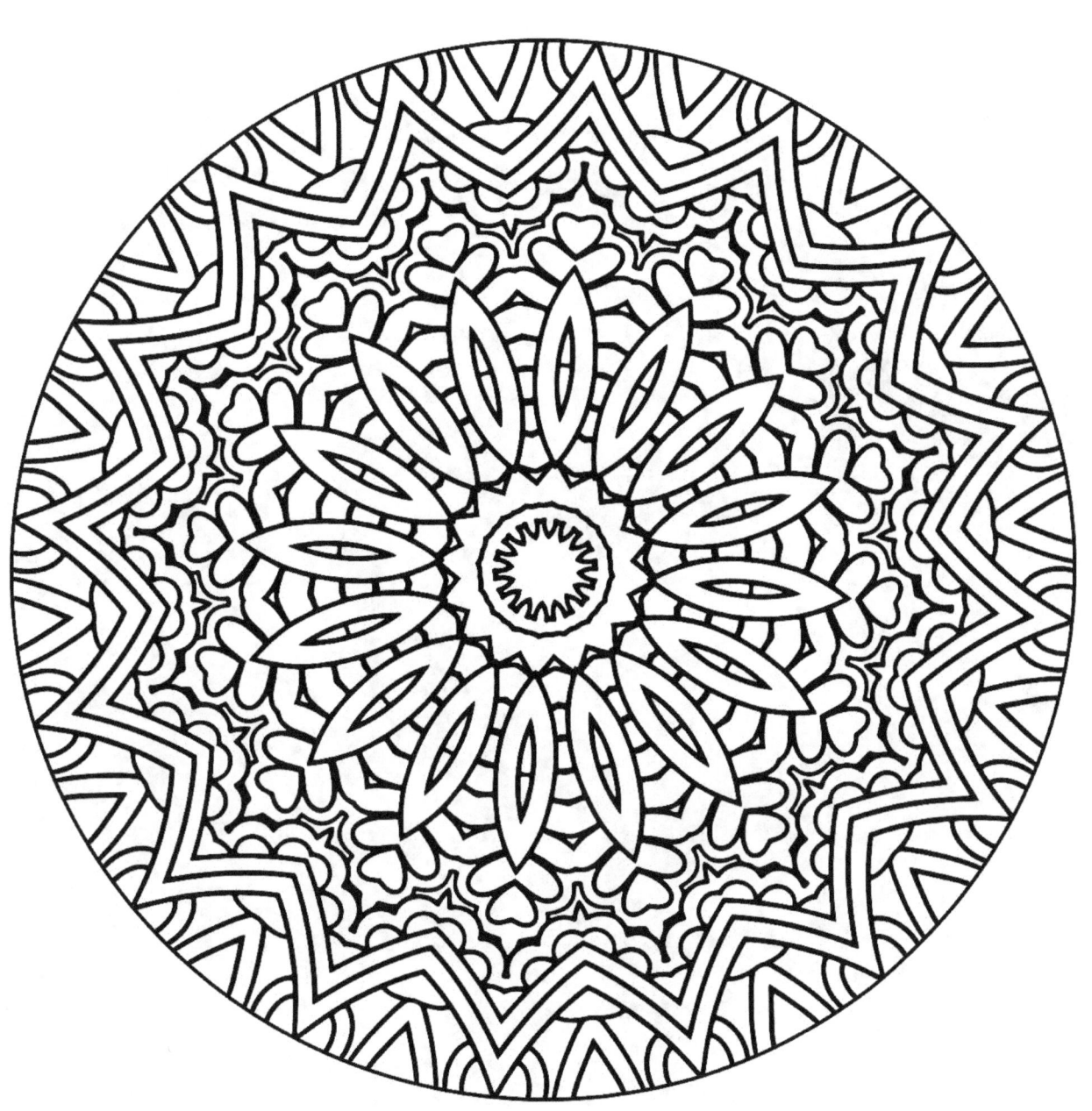

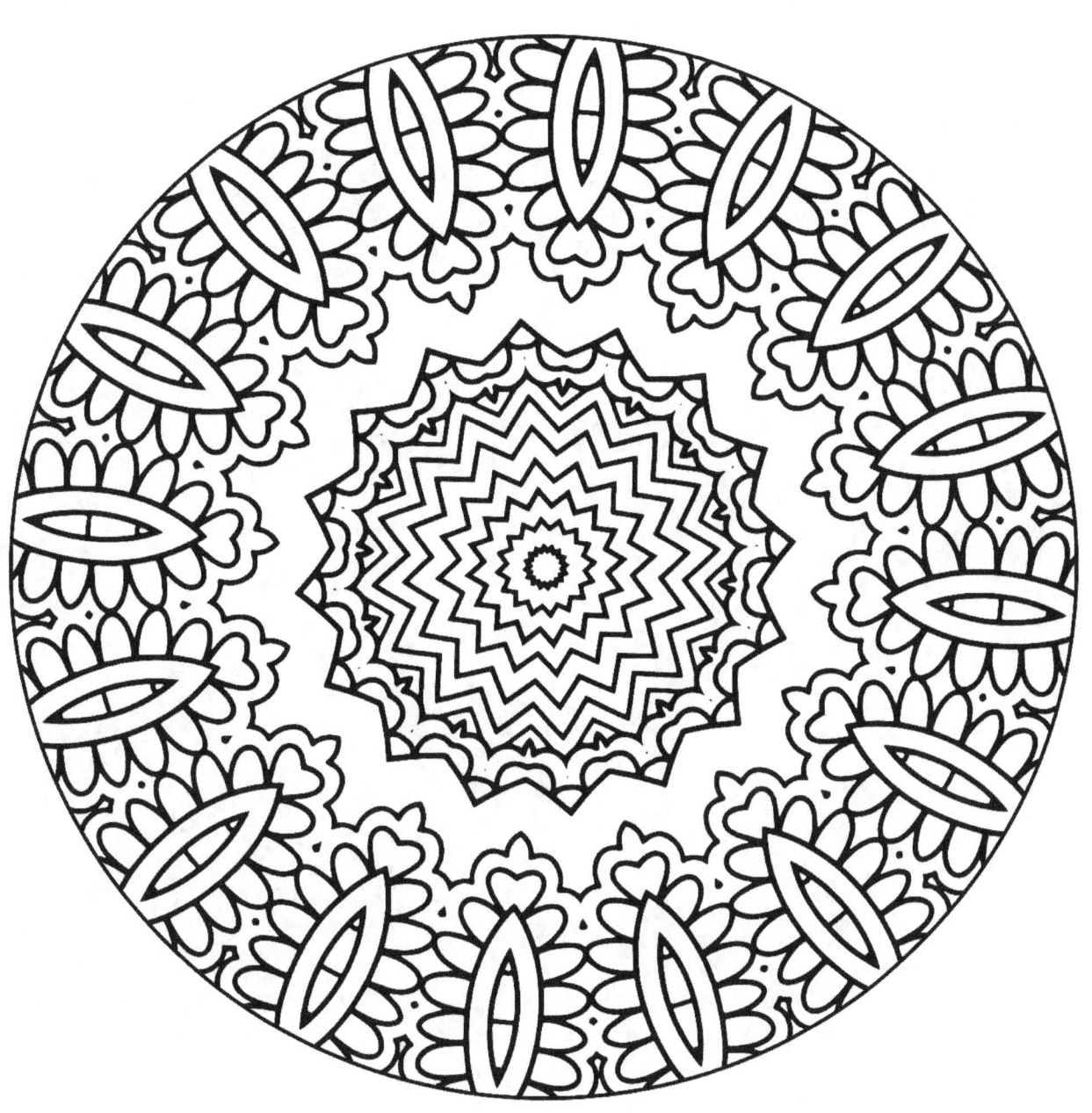

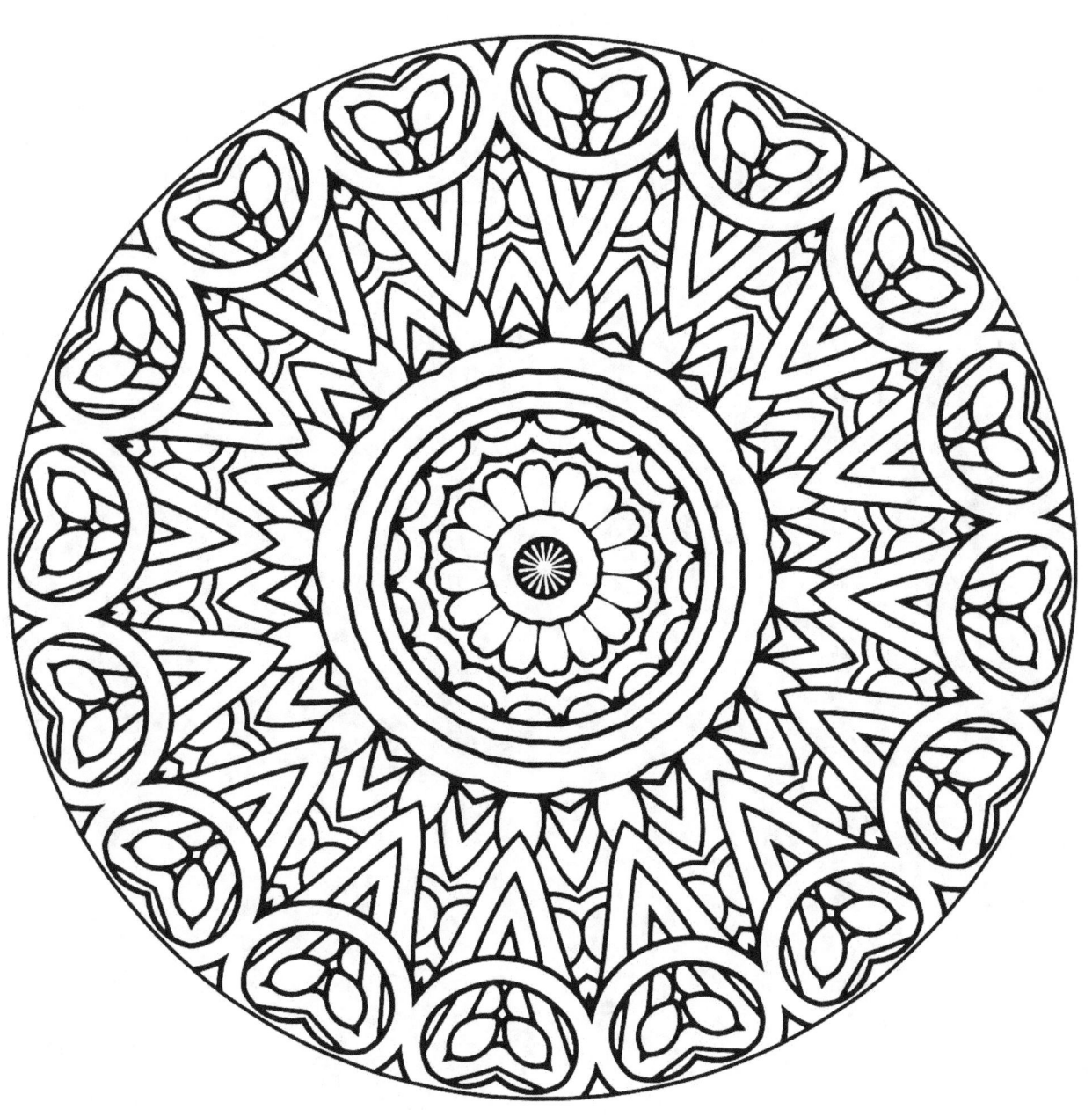

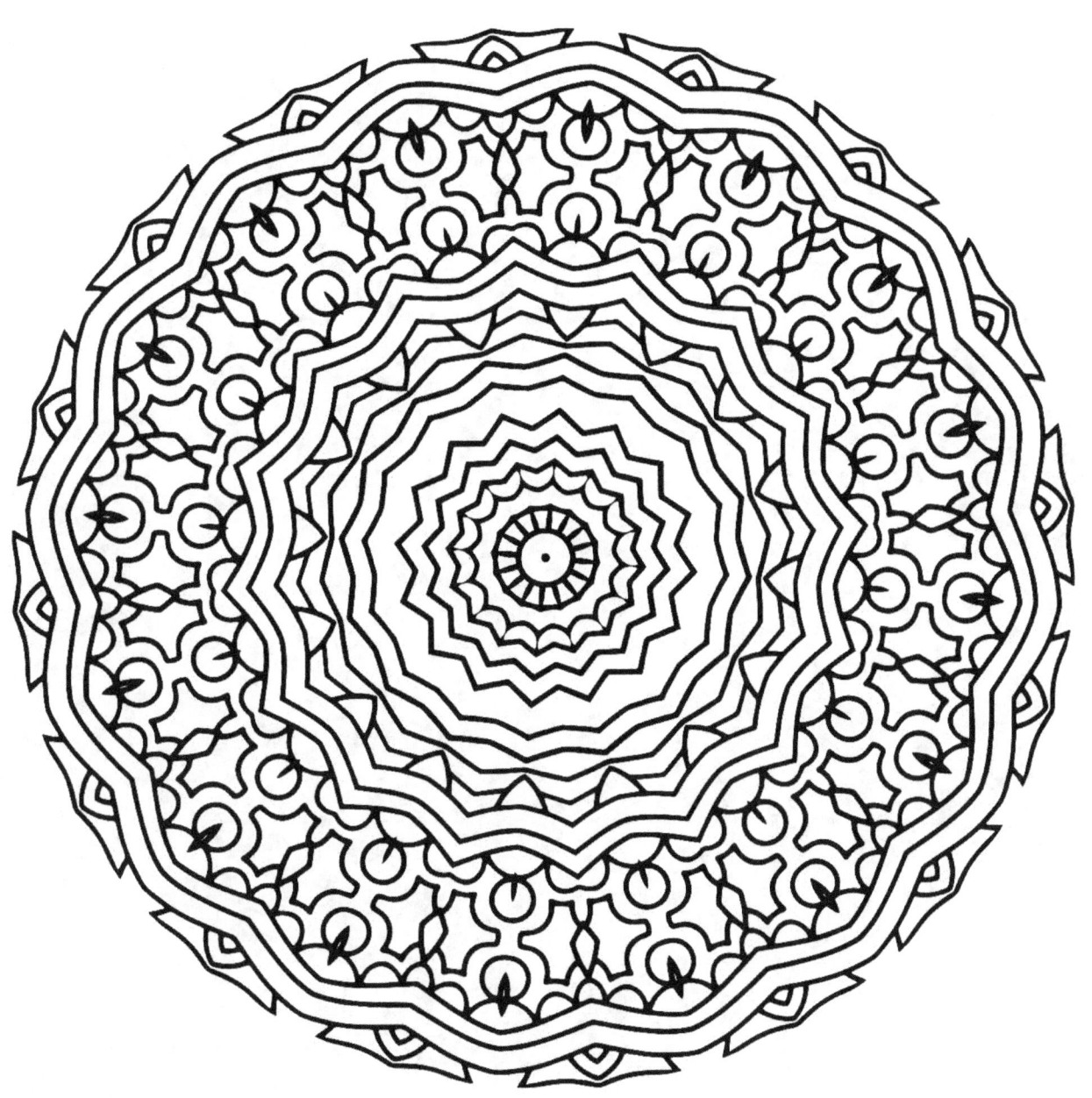

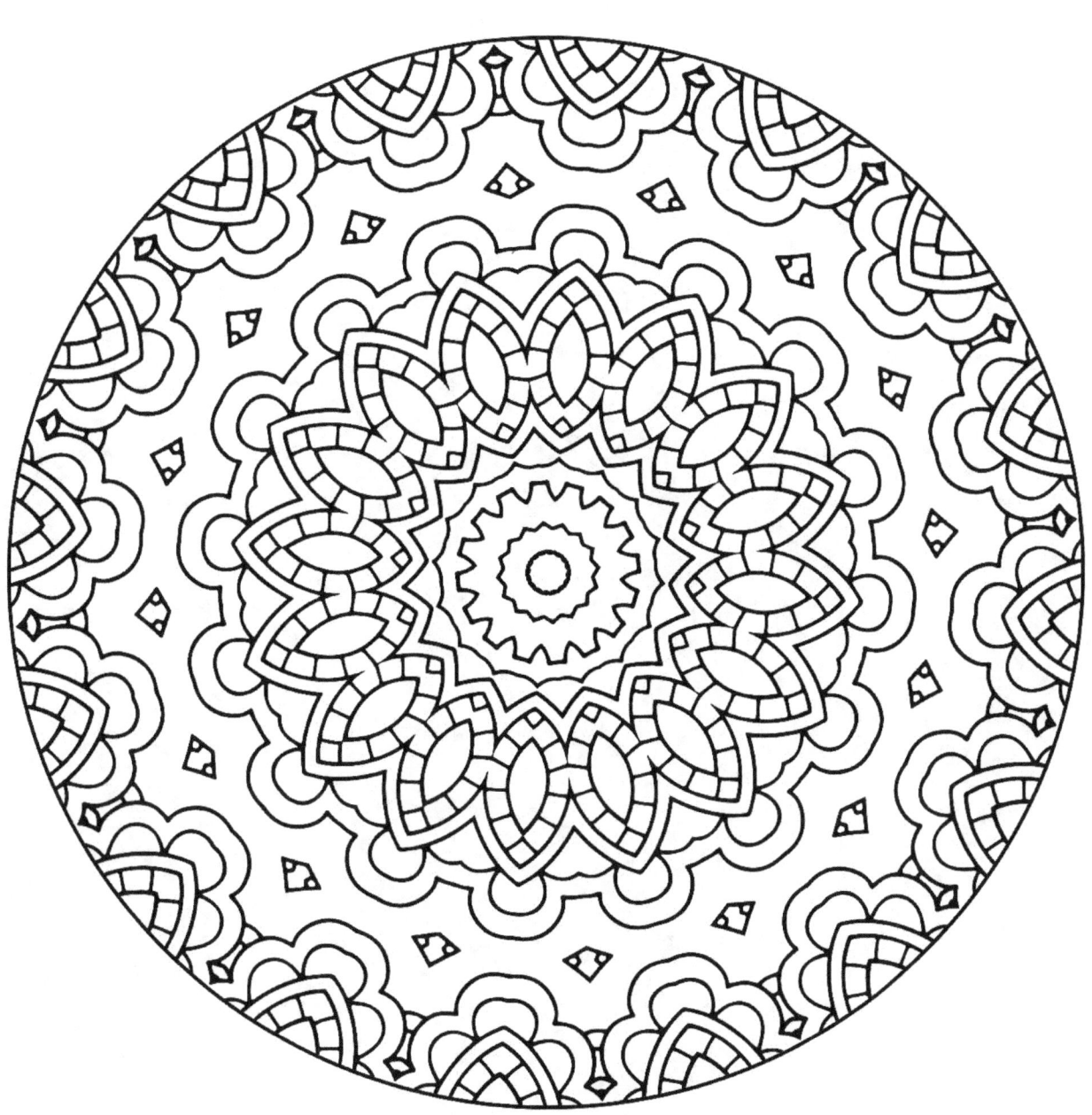

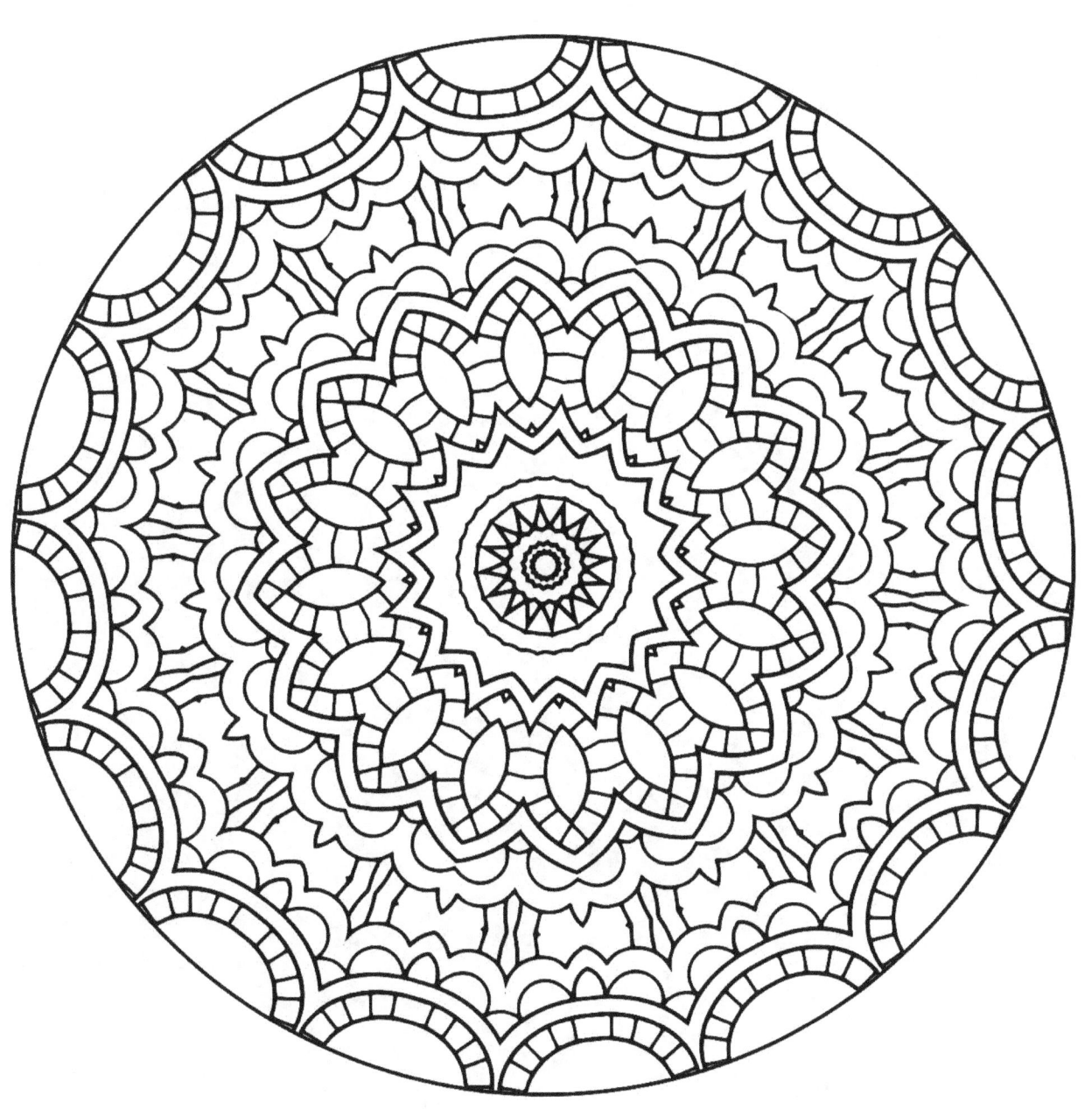

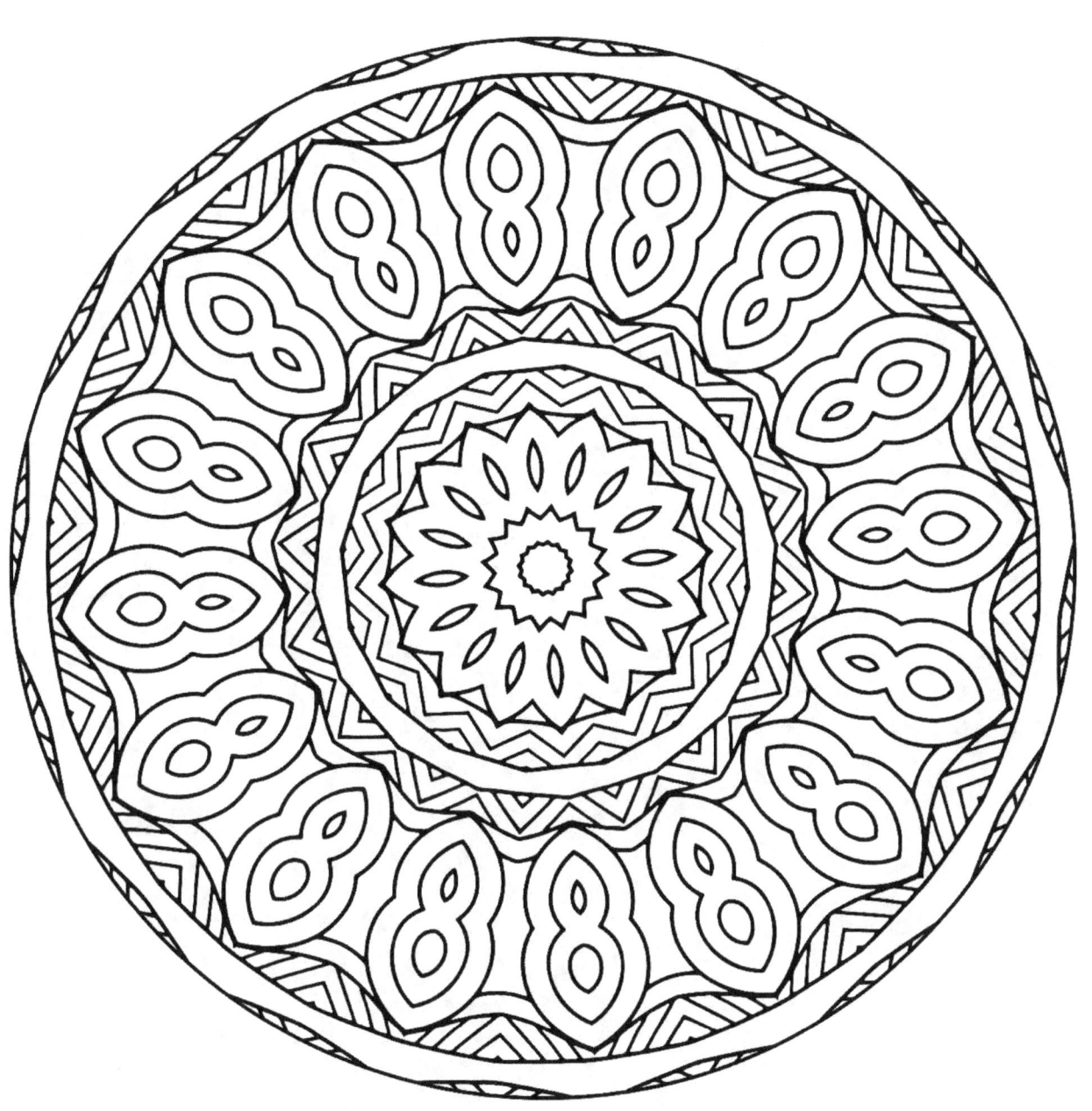

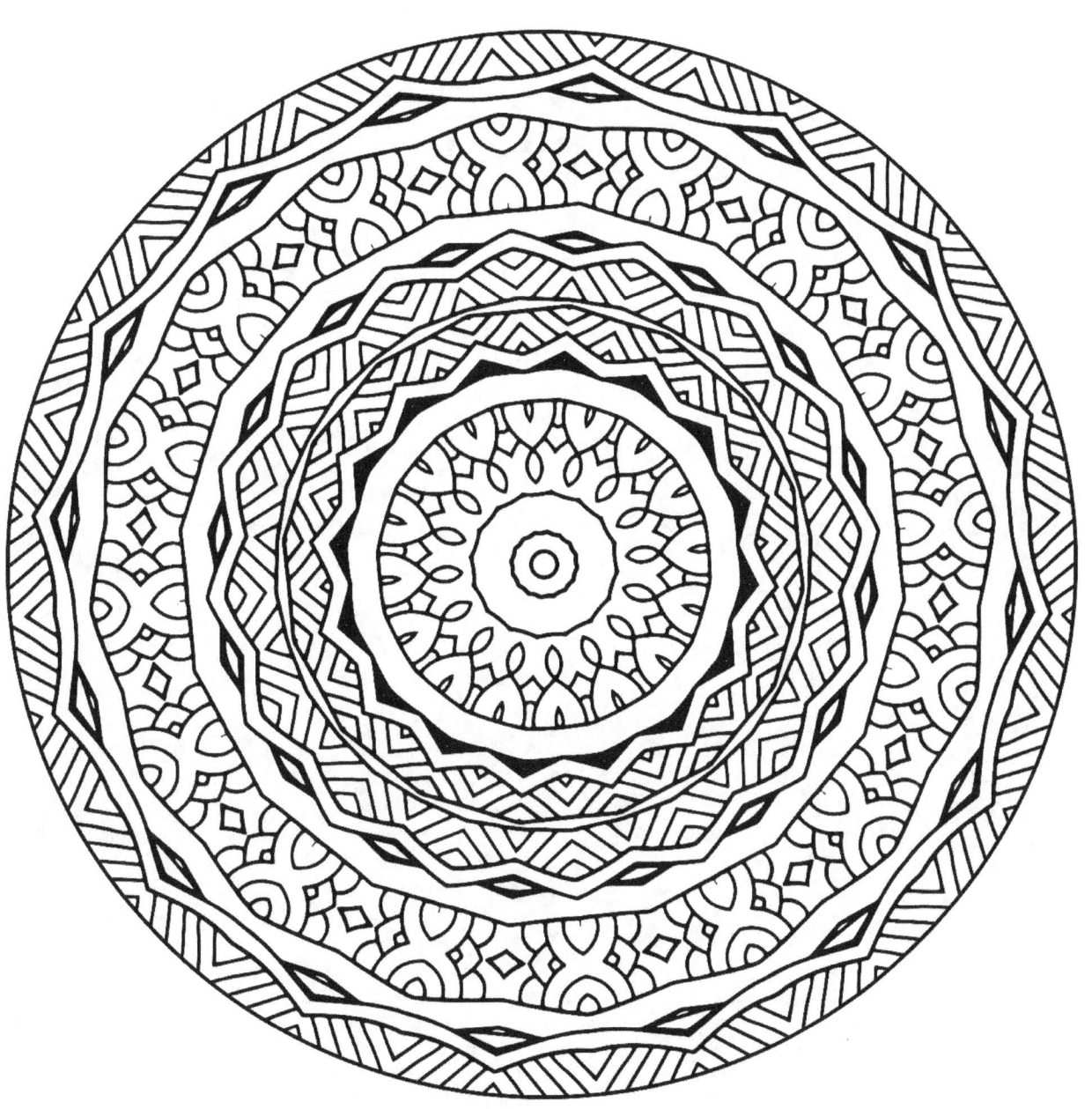

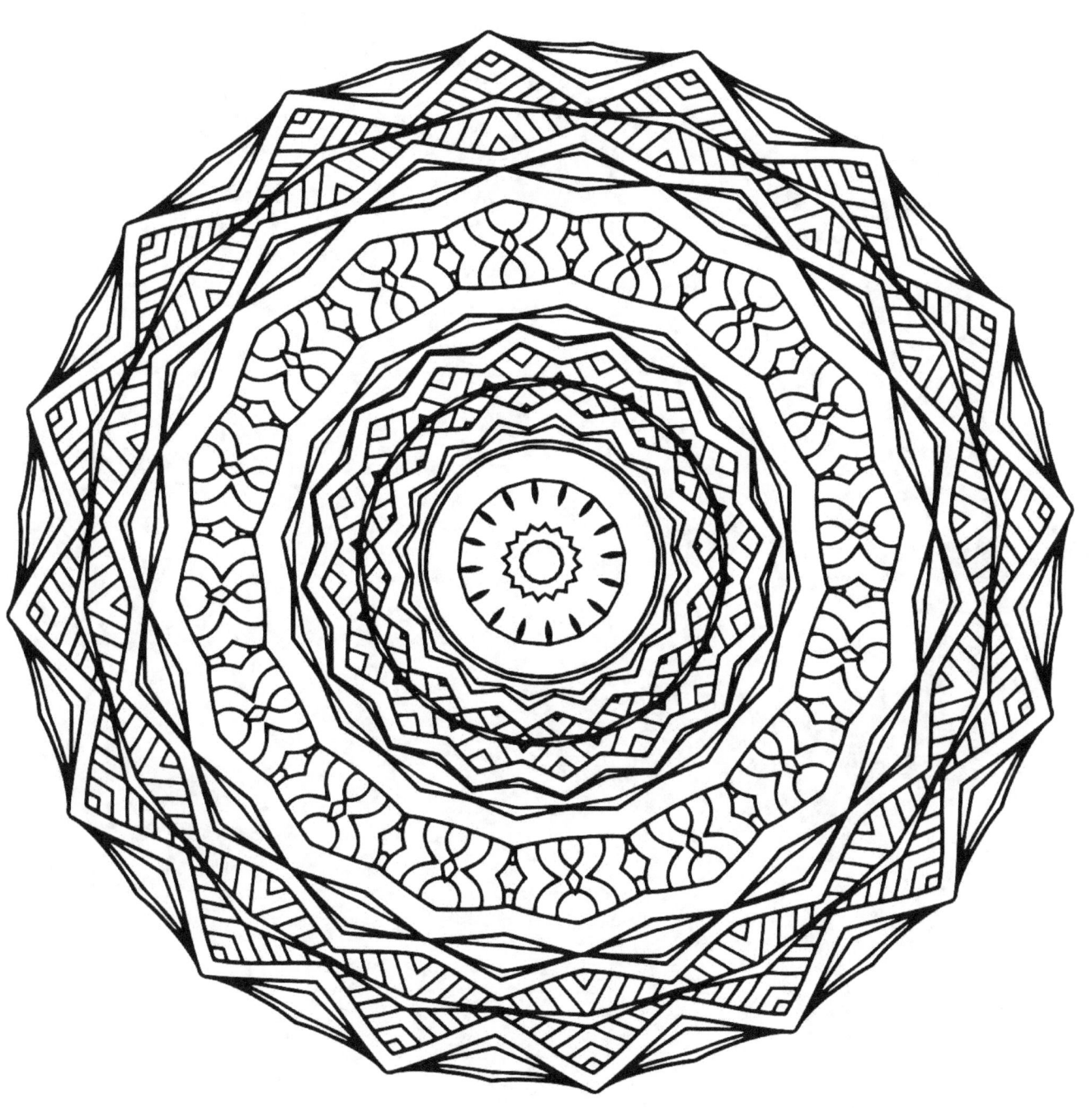

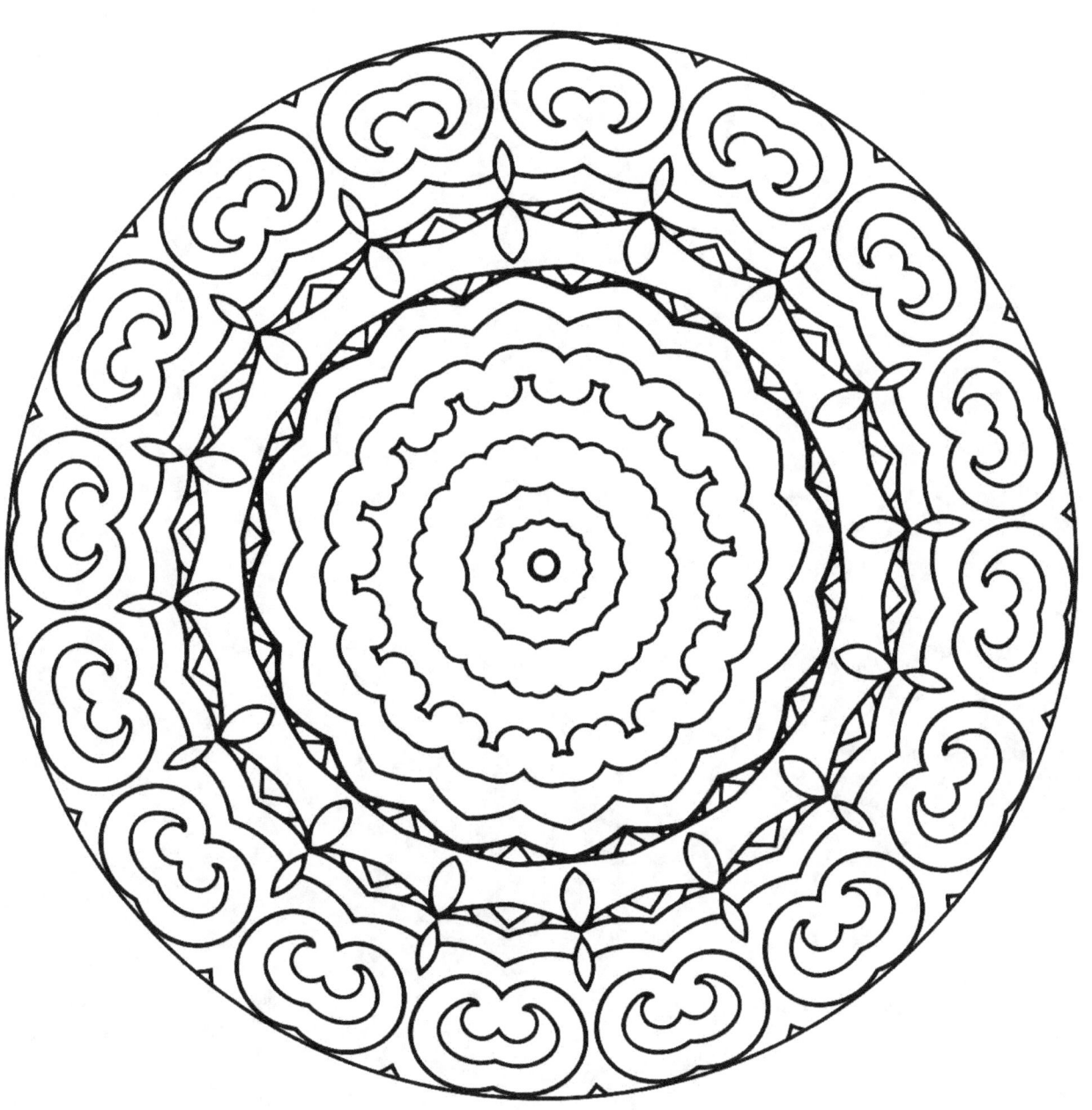

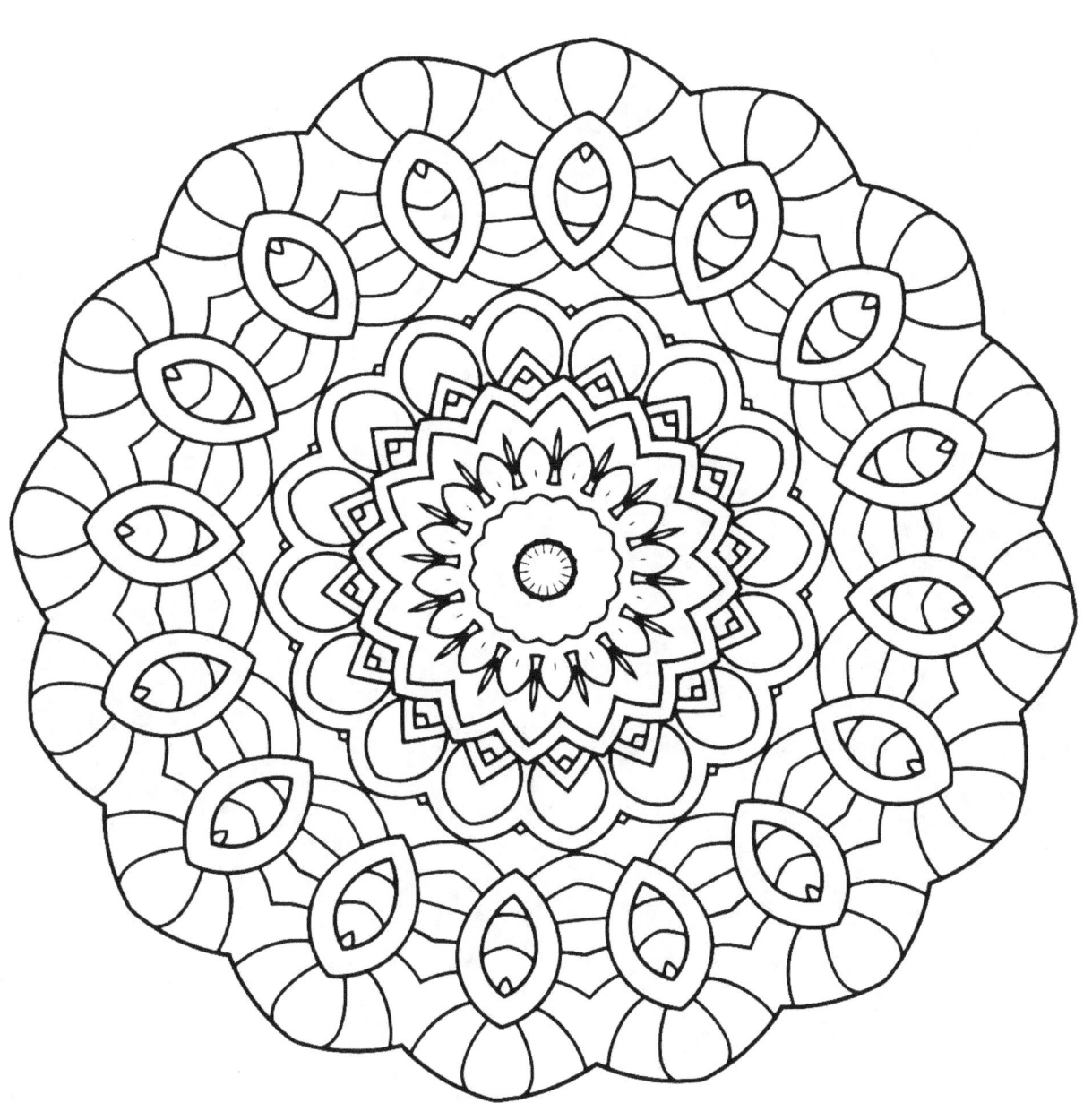

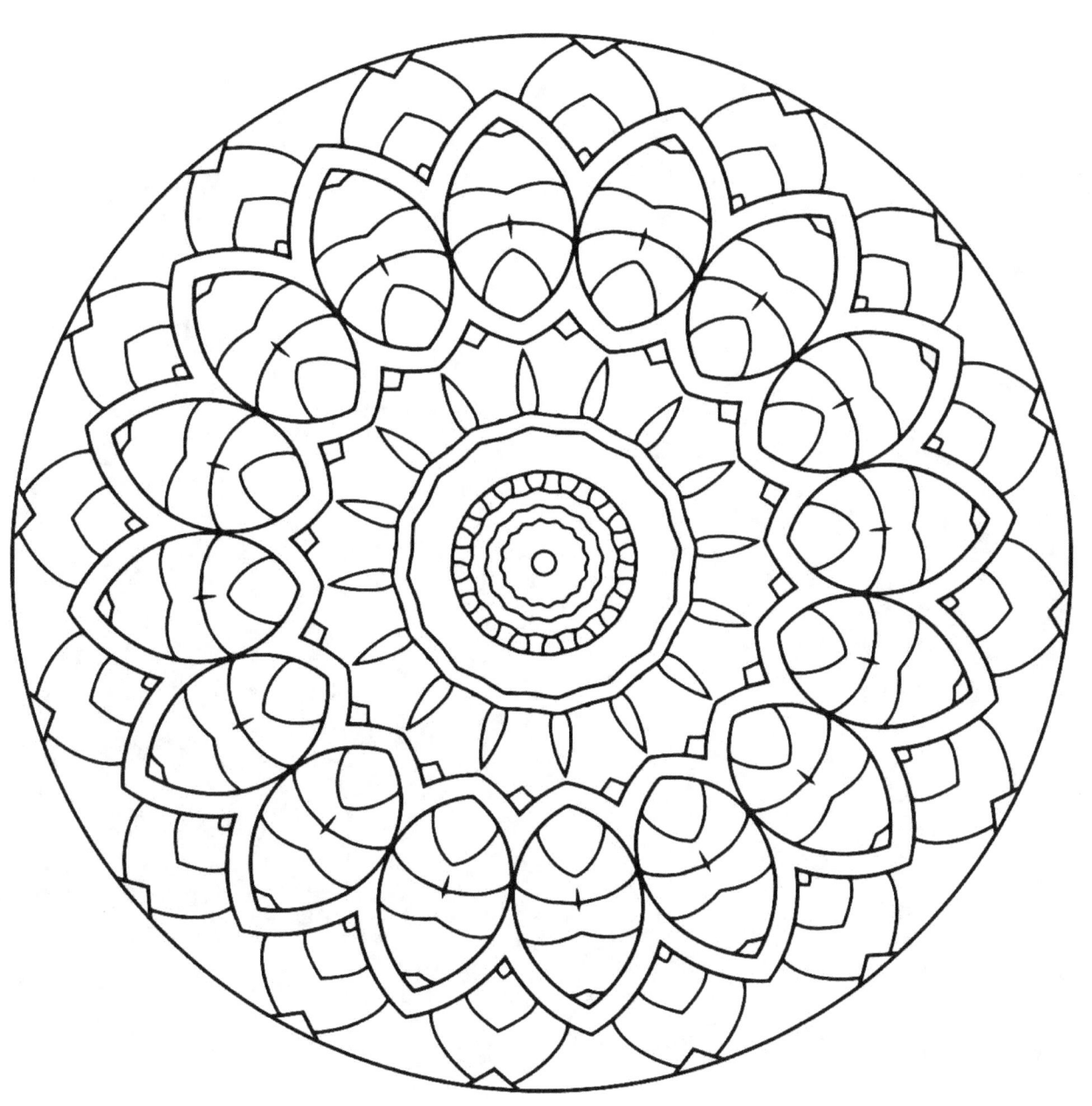

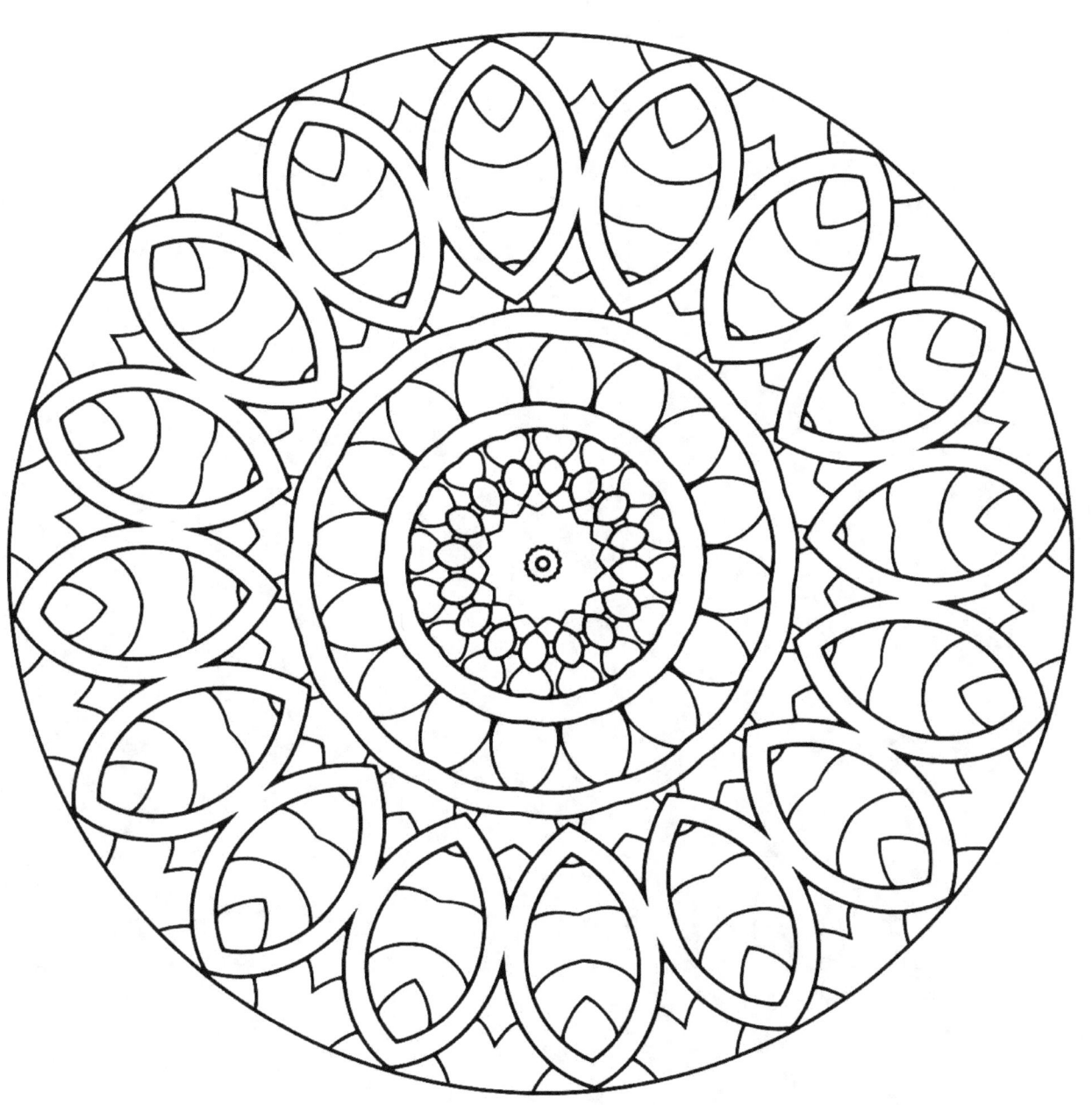

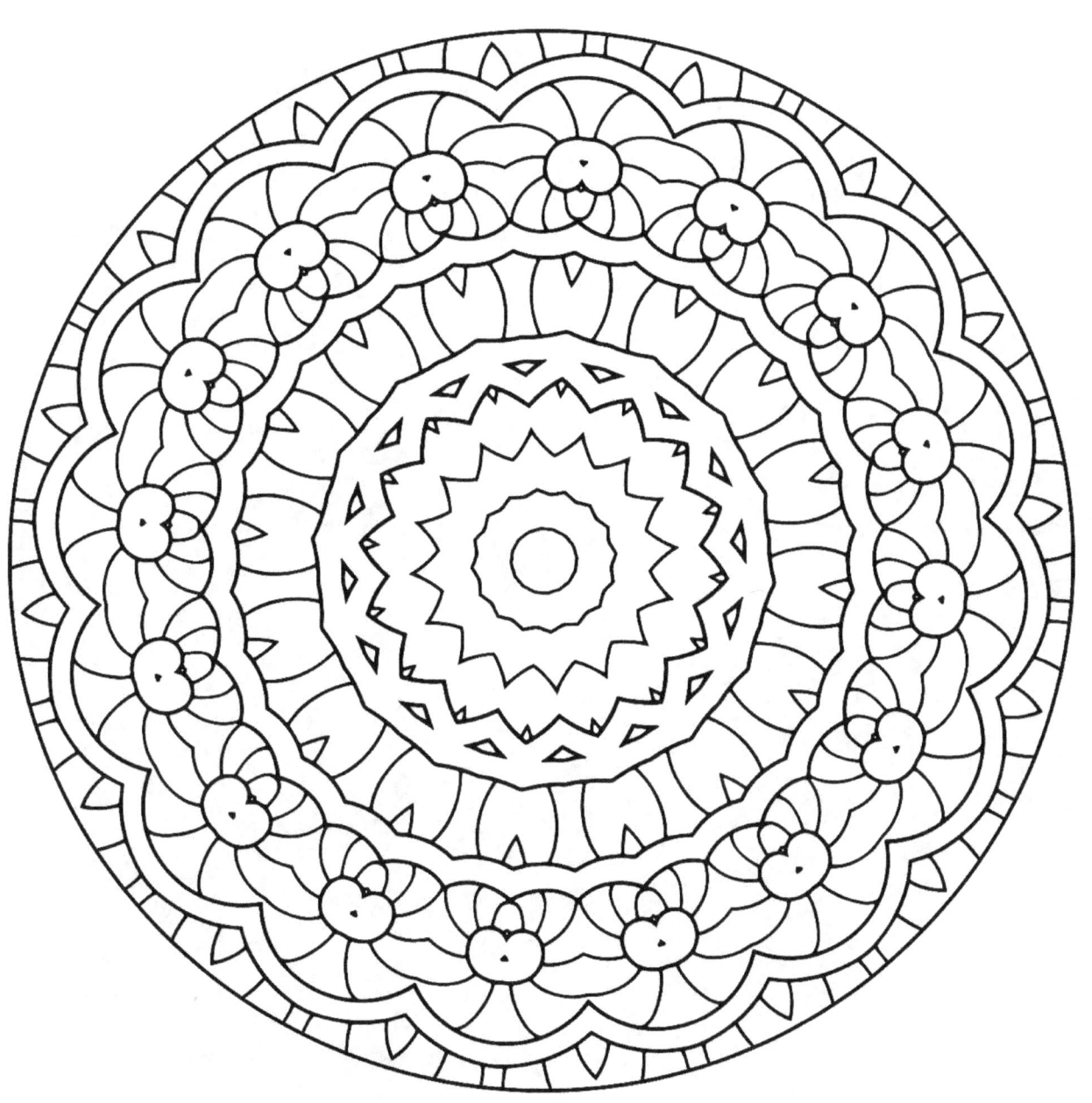

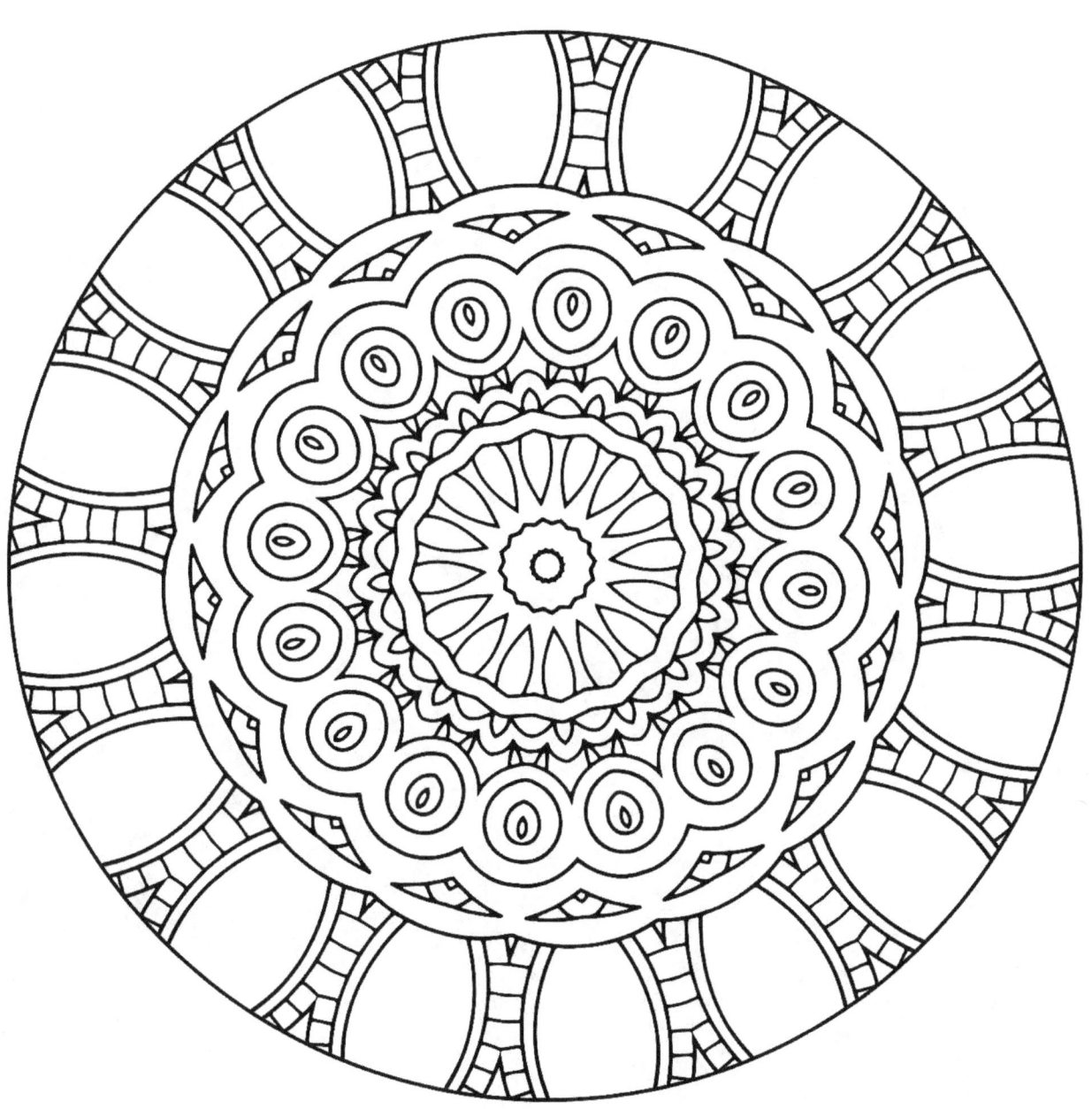

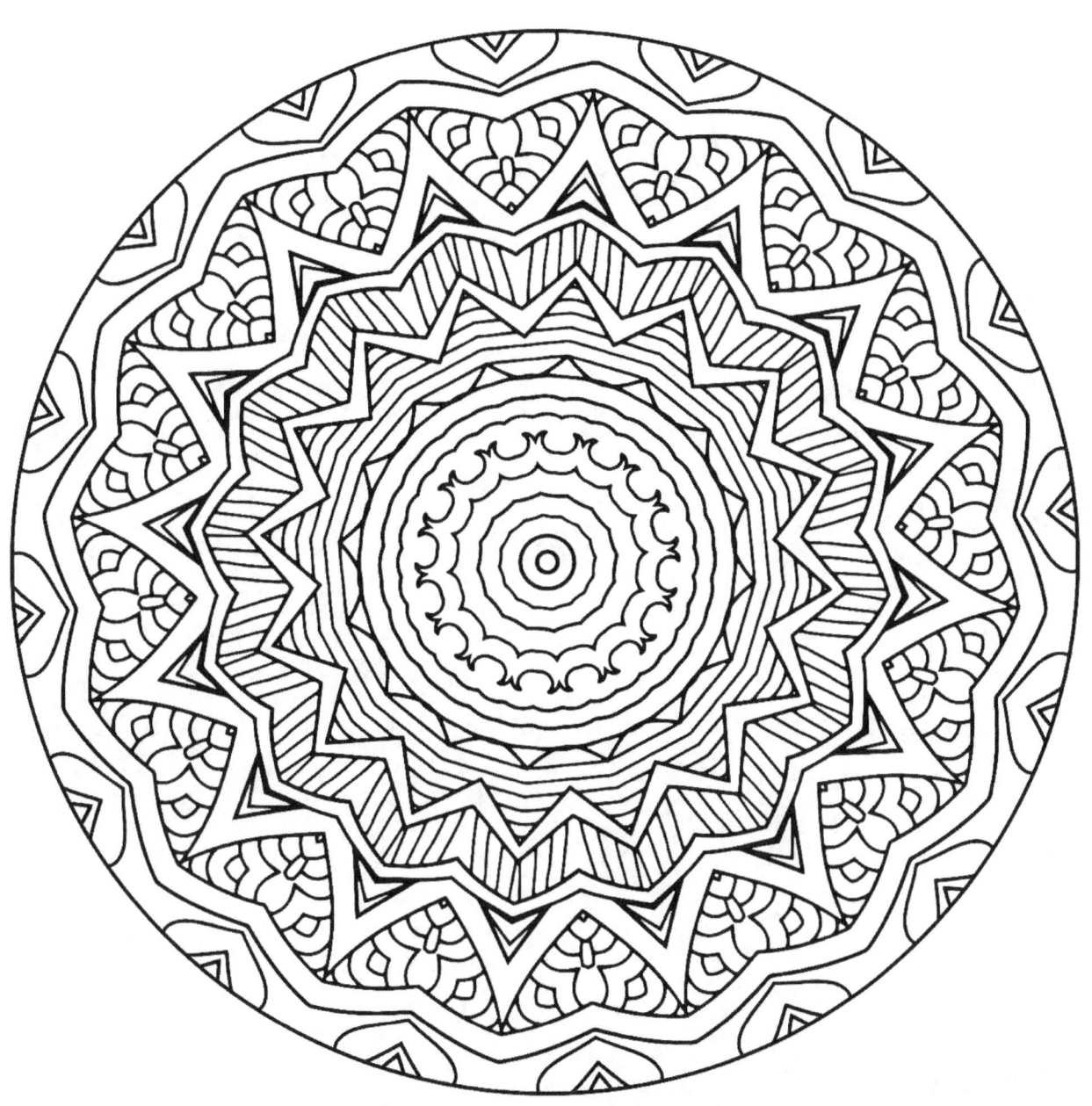

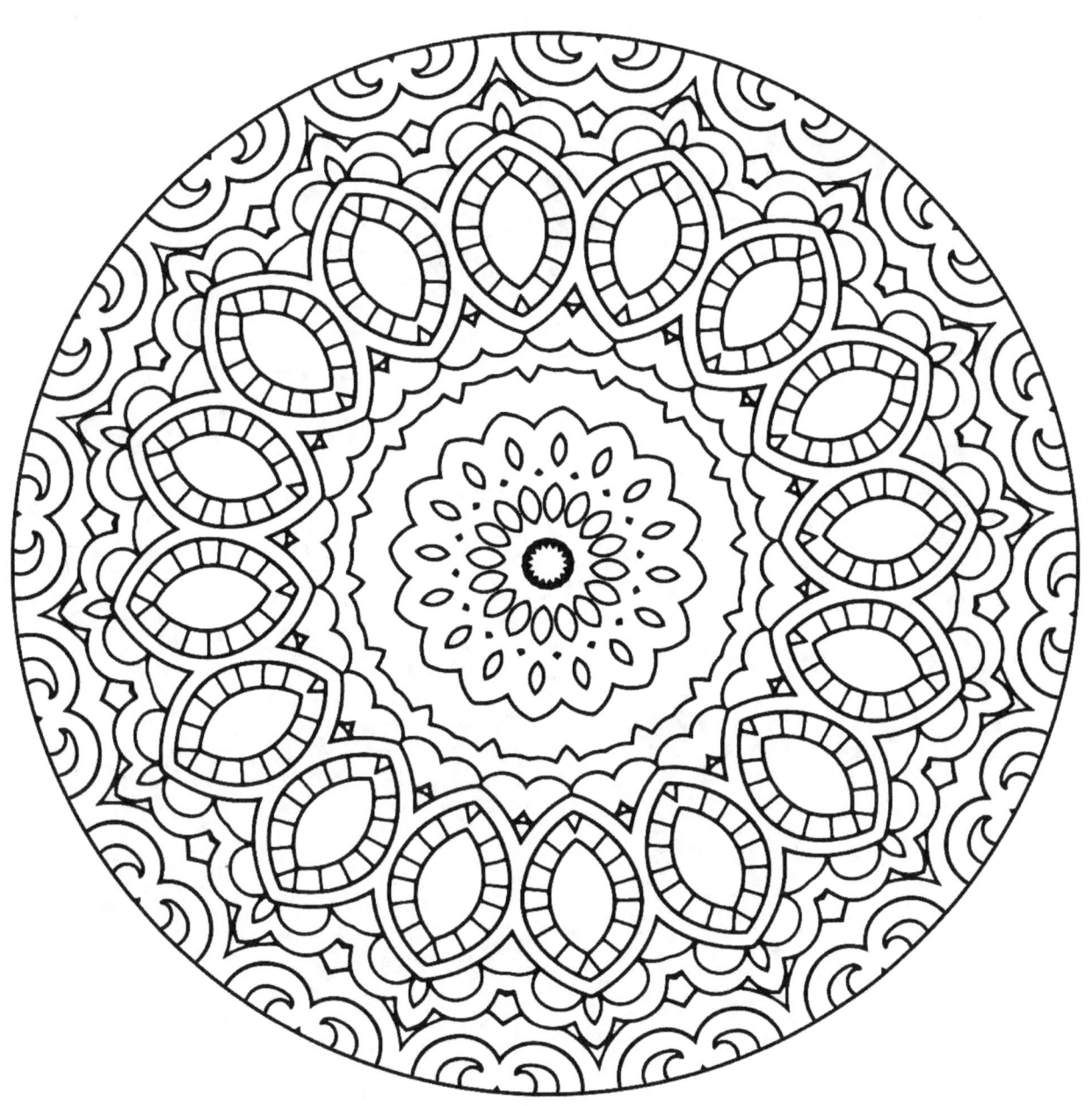

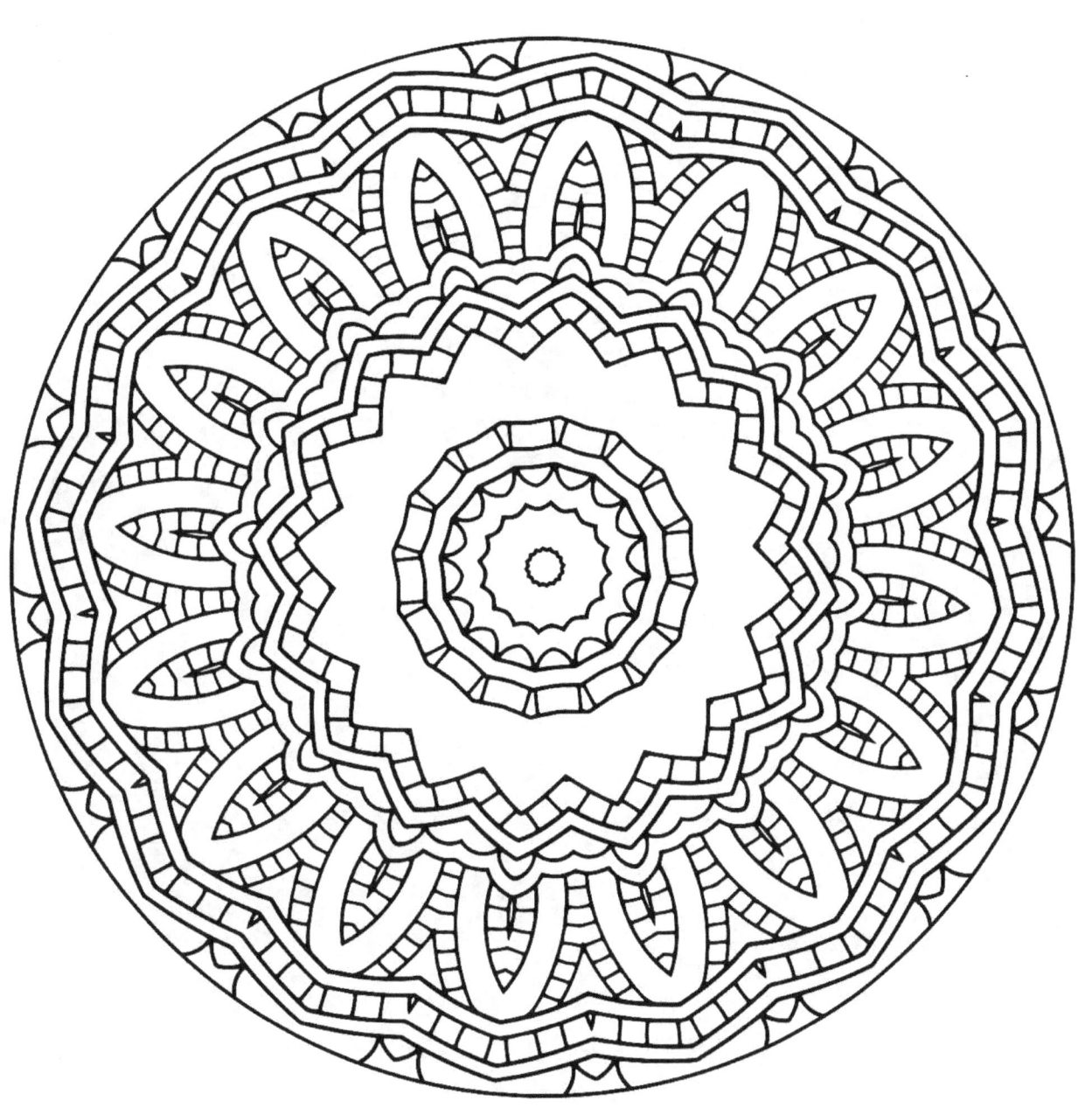

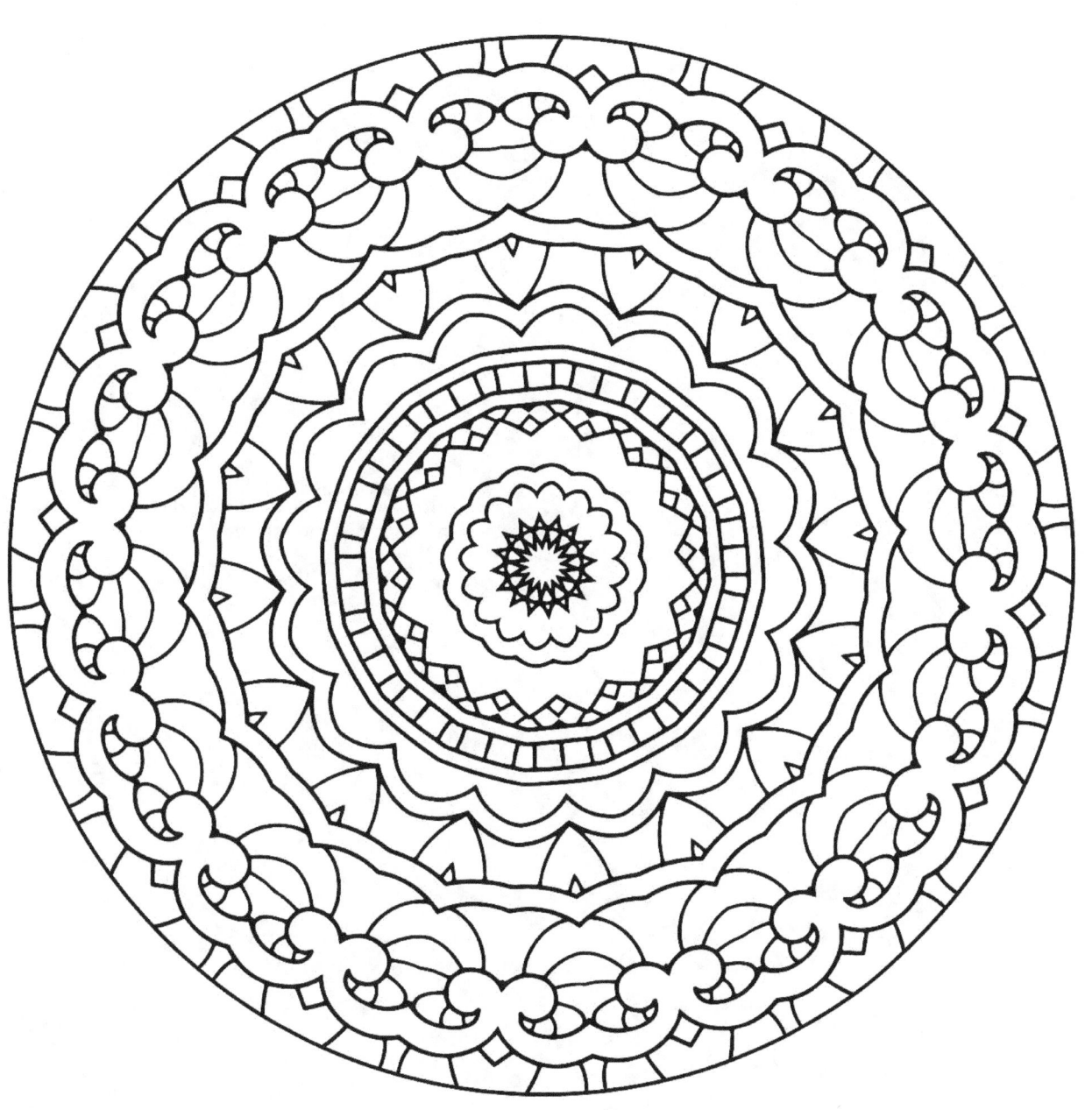

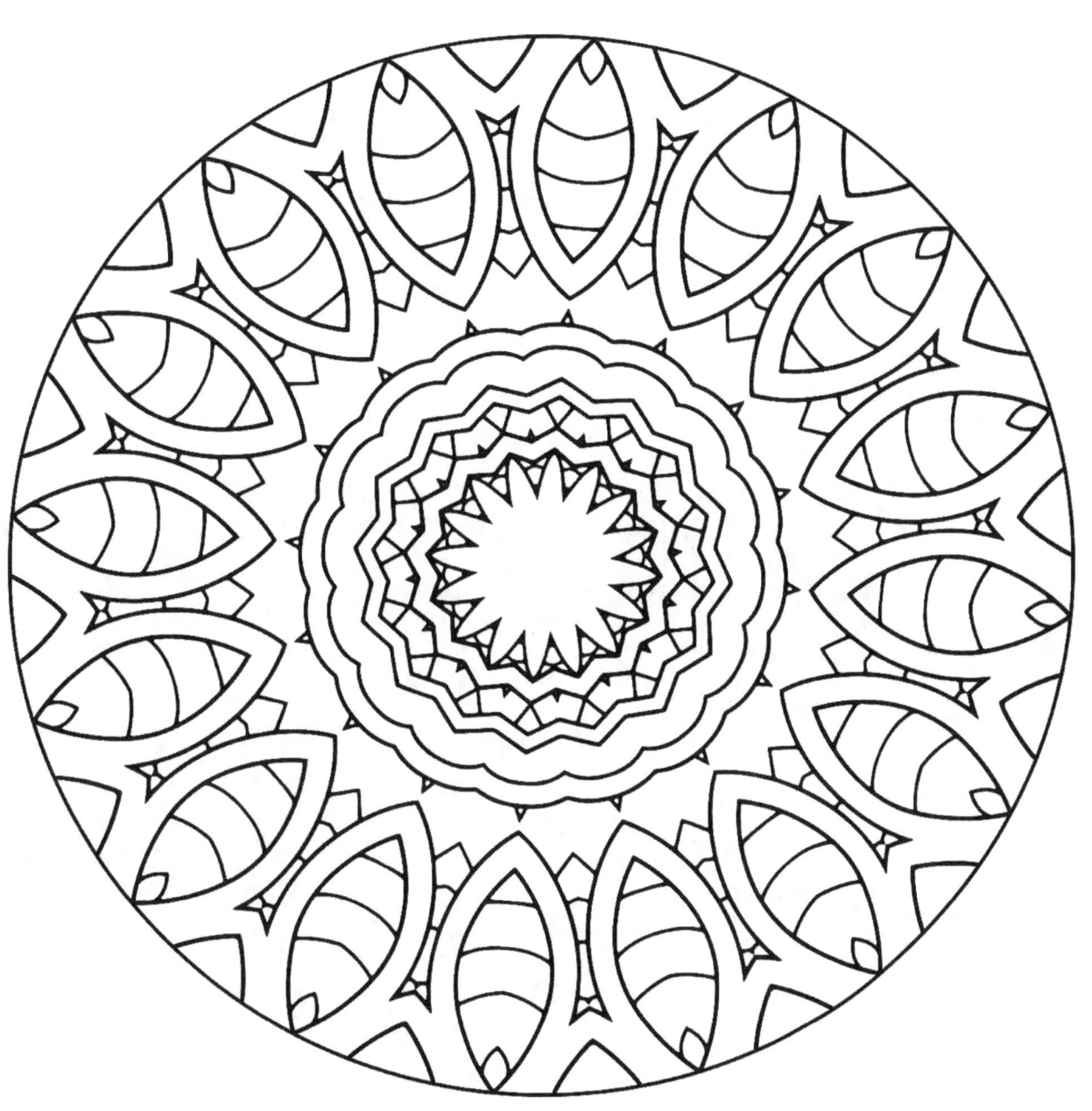

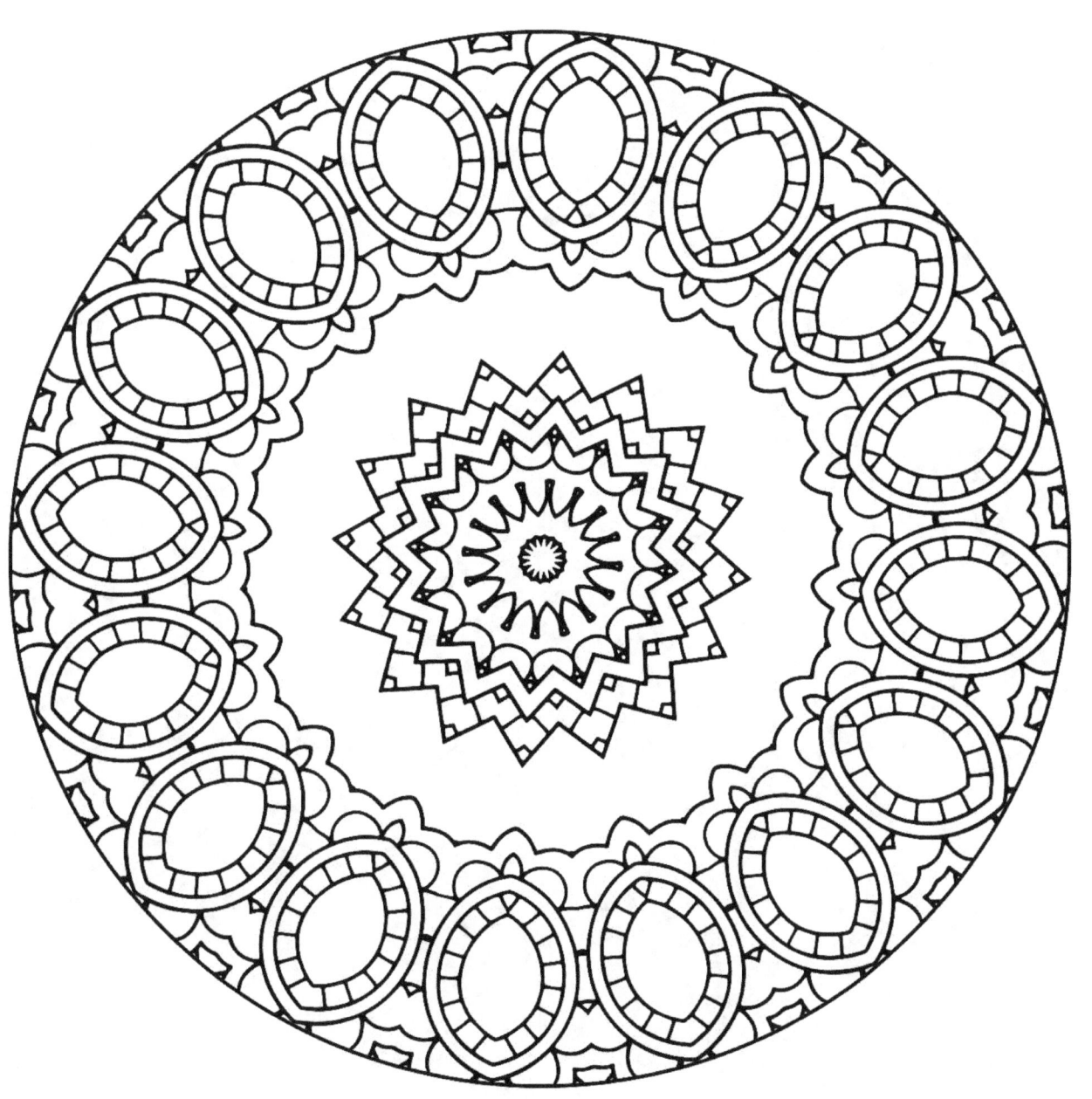

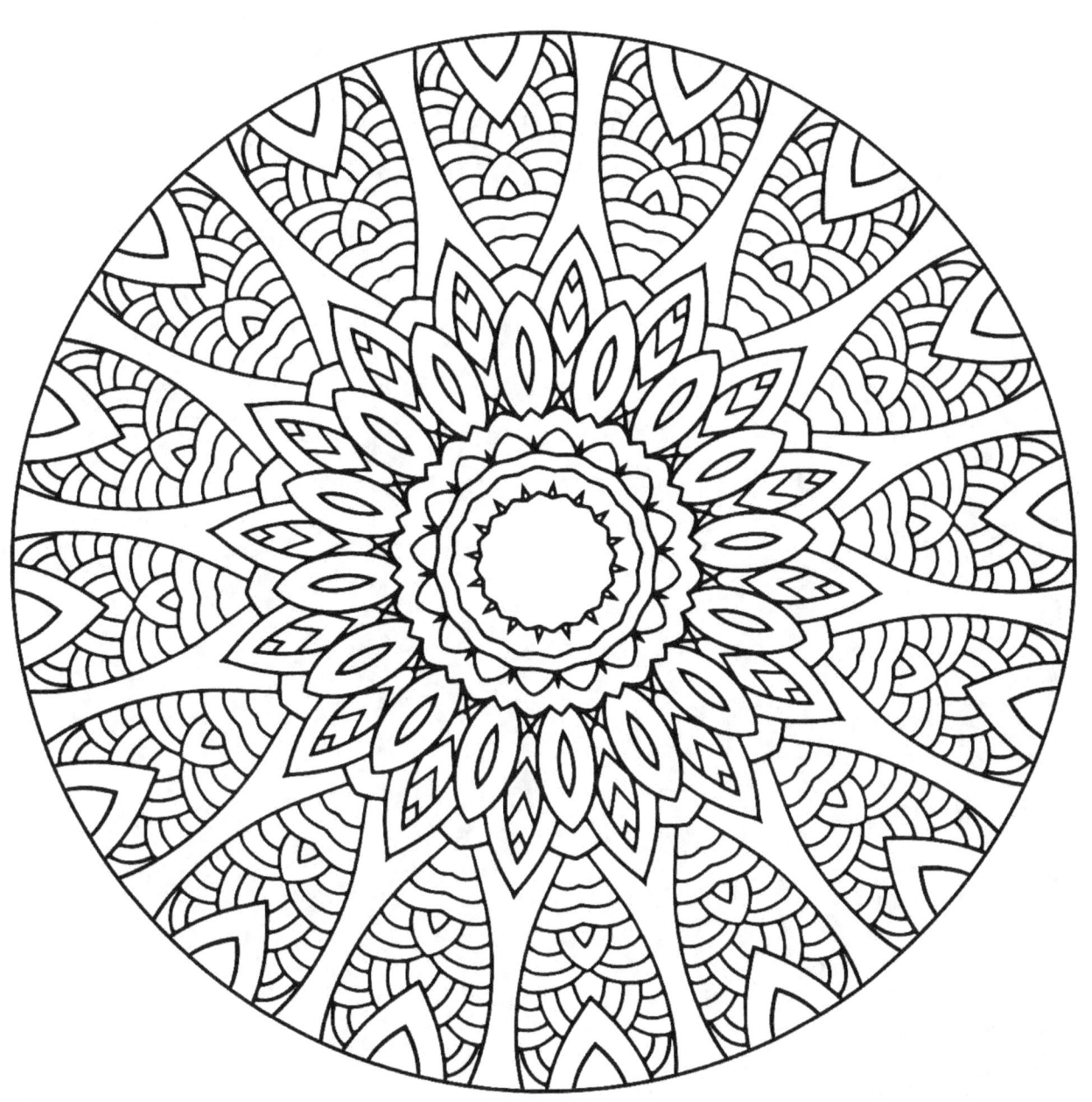

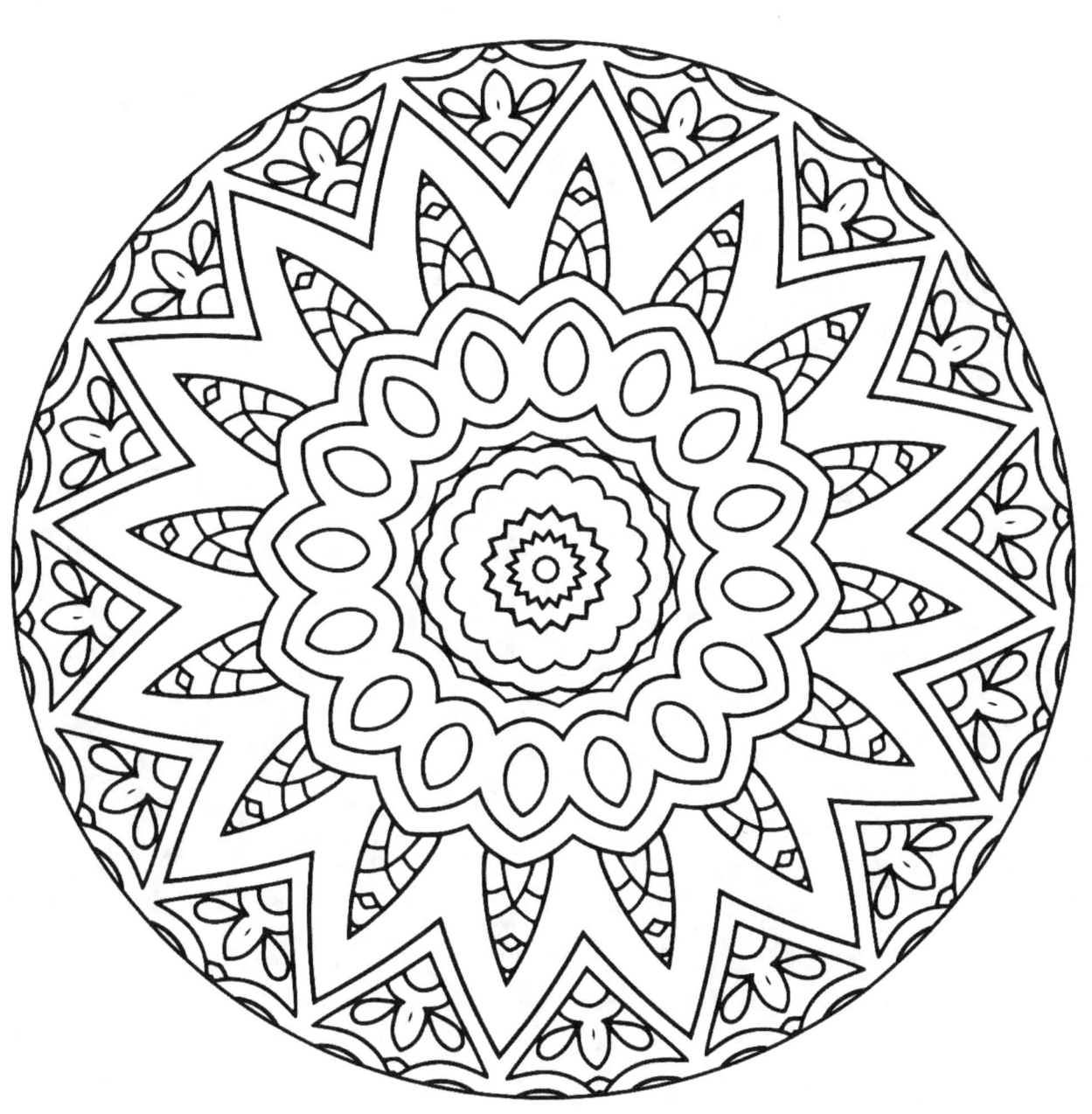

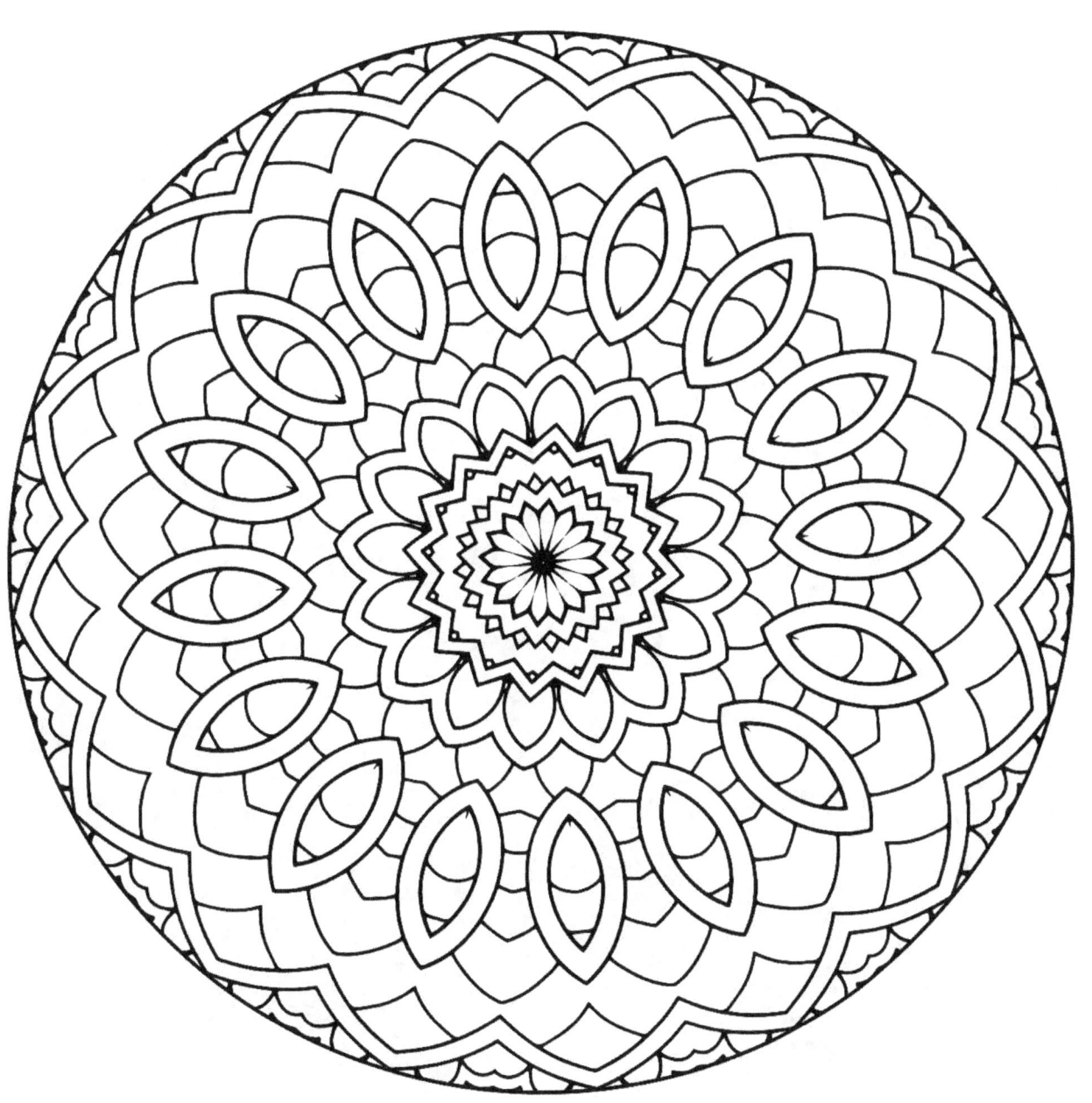

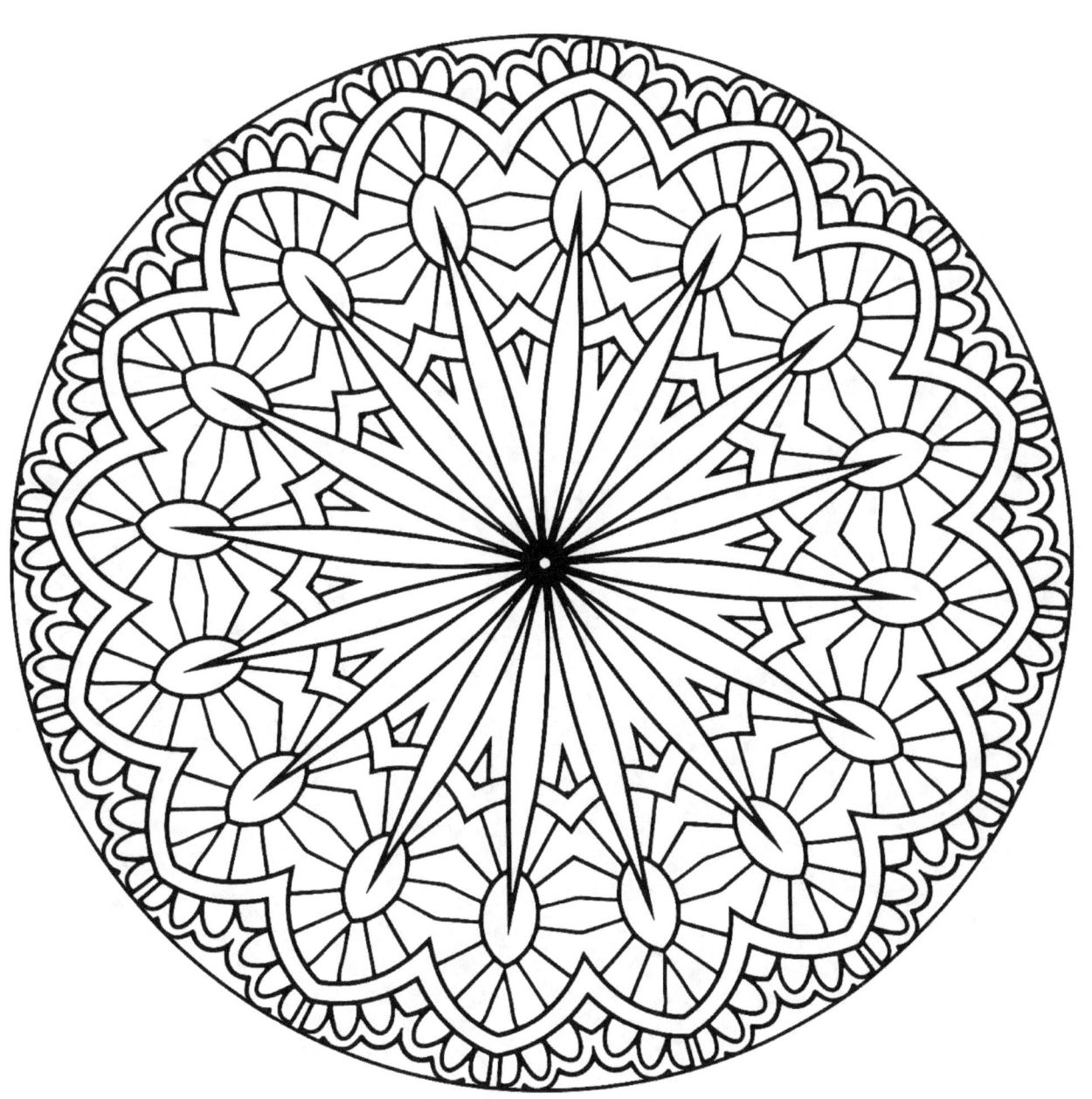

Conclusion

Thanks for all your hard work! I hope you truly enjoyed this book and found plenty of time to relax, unwind and create.

It's been a pure joy to bring these designs to you from our artists at SpectraGraf. If you would like more, please visit our site @ www.SpectraGraf.com where you will find books, art supplies, our exclusive coloring guide with color wheel and so much more!

You can also join our membership program there where you'll find a forum of like-minded artists from newbies to veterans – Everyone loves to color! Each week, members can download a new design from one of our many series.

You'll also find our SpectraShop where you can purchase all your books and supplies at members-only discounts.

Check there for contest dates when you can enter your completed artwork for a chance to win great prizes!

Go there NOW!

www. 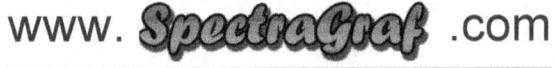 .com

Now Available from **SpectraGraf:**

Pattern Power series – Volumes 1 thru 4

Mystic Mandalas series – Volumes 1 thru 3

Paisley Passion series – Volumes 1 thru 3

See my Amazon Author page here.

Visit me on Facebook at   https://facebook.com/spectragraf

Check out my tweets at   https://twitter.com/spectragraf

Pin to my boards at   https://pinterest.com/kennethrhorn

Look at me on Instagram

www.ingramcontent.com/pod-product-compliance
Lightning Source LLC
Chambersburg PA
CBHW080832170526
45158CB00009B/2554